SUN SNOW
STARS SKY

P9-CRK-678

PUFFIN BOOKS
Published by the Penguin Group
Penguin Books USA Inc., 375 Hudson Street, New York, New York 10014, U.S.A.
Penguin Books Ltd, 27 Wrights Lane, London W8 5TZ, England
Penguin Books Australia Ltd, Ringwood, Victoria, Australia
Penguin Books Canada Ltd, 10 Alcorn Avenue, Toronto, Ontario, Canada M4V 3B2
Penguin Books (N.Z.) Ltd, 182-190 Wairau Road, Auckland 10, New Zealand

Penguin Books Ltd, Registered Offices: Harmondsworth, Middlesex, England

First published in Great Britain by William Heinemann Ltd.,
an imprint of Reed Children's Books, 1995
First published in the United States of America by Viking,
a division of Penguin Books USA Inc., 1995
Published in Puffin Books, 1997

1 3 5 7 9 10 8 6 4 2

Copyright © Catherine and Laurence Anholt, 1995
All rights reserved

THE LIBRARY OF CONGRESS HAS CATALOGED THE VIKING EDITION
UNDER CATALOG CARD NUMBER: 94-61278

Puffin Books ISBN 0-14-055824-1

Printed and bound in HongKong
Produced by Mandarin Offset

Except in the United States of America, this book is sold subject
to the condition that it shall not, by way of trade or otherwise,
be lent, re-sold, hired out, or otherwise circulated without the
publisher's prior consent in any form of binding or cover other than
that in which it is published and without a similar condition including
this condition being imposed on the subsequent purchaser.

SUN SNOW STARS SKY

Catherine and Laurence Anholt

PUFFIN BOOKS

Early in the morning the sun comes up.

Look out of your window. Is it...

frosty,

foggy,

wet,

windy,

hot,

hailing,

stormy,

snowing?

What's the weather like today?

On HOT days...

bees buzz,

tired dogs search for shade,

ice tastes nice.

Plants need a drink, too.

We don't wear many clothes,

and everyone likes to be outdoors.

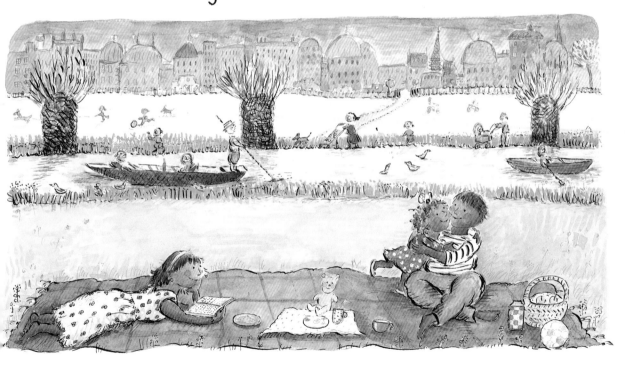

What do you do on HOT days?

Do you watch the clouds sail by
in all shapes and sizes?

What else do you see in the sky?

On COLD days...

puddles turn
to ice,

cars are hard
to start.

We have
warm drinks

and wear
lots of clothes.

We can see our breath in the air.

We might find footprints in the snow.

What do you do on COLD days?

Some animals sleep all winter.
That's called hibernating.

Other animals like the cold.

Some birds stay in the garden.

Others fly away to warmer places.

Some countries are very hot.

Others are always cold.

Some animals live only where it's hot.

Here are some of those animals.
Do you know their names?

SPRING is the time for...

lambs and chicks,

eggs in nests,

sudden showers,

buds on trees.

SUMMER is the time for...

butterflies floating,

flowers growing,

long, lazy picnics,

and vacations at the beach.

AUTUMN is the time for...

falling leaves,

fruit on trees,

harvest days,

bonfires,

berries, nuts, and squirrels.

WINTER is the time for...

skating, sledding, and snowball fights,

bare branches, gloves and scarves,

whistling winds, and glowing fires.

People say funny things about the weather.

Rain, rain, go away. Come again another day.

Red sky at night, sailors' delight.
Red sky in the morning, sailors' warning.

If the cows are lying down,
it's going to rain.

The north wind doth blow,
and we shall have snow.

Do you know any weather rhymes?

If the sun shines when it's raining, sometimes you can see a rainbow in the sky.

What do you do on a WET day?

It's fun to watch the weather change.
But what happens if there's too much...

rain,

sun,

wind,

or snow?

Whatever the weather is like,

it gets dark at the end of each day.

Night animals go hunting.

On clear nights the moon and
stars light up the sky.

What will the weather be tomorrow?

Other Picture Books from Puffin for the Very Young